The Year in History
1947

Whitman Publishing, LLC

www.whitman.com

ISBN: 0794837298

Printed in China

Scan the QR code at left or visit us at www.whitman.com for a complete listing of collectibles-related books, supplies, and storage products.

Whitman®

Contents

Introduction 4

Chapter 1
Famous People Born in 1947 6

Chapter 2
The Cost of Living in 1947 14

Chapter 3
Day-by-Day Calendar of 1947 20

Chapter 4
Pop Culture in 1947 112

Credits and Acknowledgments 120

Introduction

By 1947 the veterans who returned from World War II two years earlier had settled into their post-war lives, either finding jobs or attending college under the GI Bill. This led to an unprecedented 30-year run of prosperity, giving families plenty of leisure time and spending money. The baby boom, as it became known, was underway.

The rest of the world, however, did not adjust as well to post-war life. Europe was in tatters from the destruction, and many countries struggled to rebuild. Soviet Premier Joseph Stalin saw an opportunity to extend the Communist Bloc beyond the Eastern European countries they had taken over during the war. To prevent the spread of Communism, President Truman proposed the Truman Doctrine, which provided economic and military aid to Greece and Turkey, both of whom were vulnerable to a Soviet takeover. This decision was seen in retrospect as the start of the Cold War, which would dominate American foreign policy for the next 45 years.

With the American economy booming, the Marshall Plan, named for Secretary of State George Marshall, was proposed in March to provide financial assistance to every European country that requested it. By the time the program ended in 1951, 18 countries, including our former enemies Germany, Italy, and Austria, had received an estimated total of over $12 billion in aid.

The British Empire, which was starting to fall apart in the years before World War II, became even weaker in the face of their economic problems. By the middle of 1947, they were prepared to pull out of India, and devised a partition that created the independent nations of India and Pakistan in August. But disputes over the territories of Jammu and Kashmir led to a war between the new countries two months later.

Similarly, Britain also found themselves in an untenable situation in Palestine. Unable to devote their attention to both India and Palestine, they asked the United Nations to determine the fate of the territory, which led to the creation of the State of Israel in 1948.

Back in America, the country enjoyed its newfound prosperity, but not without its struggles. President Truman battled with Congress on many issues, most famously on the Taft-Hartley Act, which weakened labor unions and was passed by Congress over Truman's veto.

The motion picture industry continued to thrive, but the fear of Communist infiltration in Hollywood led to Congressional hearings on the subject. By the end of the year, ten writers and directors would be blacklisted for asserting their Fifth Amendment rights and refusing to testify about their knowledge of the subject.

Although the Civil Rights Movement wouldn't pick up steam until the mid-1950s, strides towards ending racial discrimination were being made, most famously when Jackie Robinson became the first African American to play in Major League Baseball when he signed with the Brooklyn Dodgers. Despite jeers from opposing crowds, problems with several teammates, and even death threats, Robinson kept his dignity, and was named baseball's first Rookie of the Year.

Newer technologies also began to affect American society in 1947. The introduction of the tubeless tire made cars safer and more efficient. The number of television stations would increase tenfold, and the end of the year would see the invention of the transistor, which would have an enormous impact in shaping our lives today. Research into computers continued following the previous year's invention of the ENIAC, the world's first electronic computer, and although they wouldn't become popular for years, 1947 saw the invention of the microwave oven and the instant camera.

News stories also captured the attention of Americans throughout 1947. A brutal murder in Los Angeles, the "Black Dahlia" case, made headlines across the country. Sightings of unidentified flying objects, most famously in Washington and New Mexico, fueled our collective interest in outer space.

It was a fascinating year, one that shaped the America, and the world, that we know today.

American zoologist Jack Hanna is born on January 2 in Knoxville, Tennessee.

Famous People Born in 1947

The second year of the post–Word War II "baby boom," 1947 saw many people who would become pop culture icons in the 1970s enter the world. Rock 'n' roll stars dominate this list, most famously David Bowie (January 8) and Elton John (March 25). Two of the founding members of the Eagles, Don Henley (July 22) and Don Felder (September 21), were born in 1947, as were Timothy B. Schmit (October 30) and Joe Walsh (November 20), both of whom would eventually join the band.

Of the athletes who were born in 1947, it was a good year for baseball catchers, with Thurman Munson (June 7) and Bob Boone (November 19). In addition, the future Hall of Fame catchers who squared off in the 1975 World Series, Johnny Bench and Carlton Fisk, were born 19 days apart (December 7 and 26, respectively).

Many actors who would later gain fame while working together on sitcoms were born in 1947, including three of the four leads of *Laverne & Shirley*—Cindy Williams (August 22), David L. Lander (June 22), and Michael McKean (October 17). Ted Danson (December 29) would star on *Cheers* with John Ratzenberger (April 6) and later join Larry David (July 2) and Richard Lewis (June 29) in the cast of *Curb Your Enthusiasm*.

One interesting coincidence: June 21, 1947, saw the birth of actors Meredith Baxter and Michael Gross. In 1982, the two would begin a seven-year run as the married couple Elyse and Steven Keaton on the hit TV series *Family Ties*.

Nolan Ryan, who would grow up to be a Major League Baseball pitcher, is born on January 31 in Refugio, Texas.

January 2—Jack Hanna, zoologist and television personality

January 5—Mercury Morris, football player

January 8—David Bowie (born David Jones), English rock musician ("Ziggy Stardust")

January 19—Paula Deen, chef and television star

January 21—Jill Eikenberry, actress *(L.A. Law)*

January 24—Warren Zevon, rock musician ("Werewolves of London")

January 31—Nolan Ryan, baseball pitcher

February 1—Jessica Savitch, journalist

February 2—Farrah Fawcett, actress *(Charlie's Angels)*

February 3—Dave Davies, guitarist, The Kinks ("You Really Got Me")

February 4—Dan Quayle, 44th vice president of the United States

February 5—Darrell Waltrip, race car driver and broadcaster

February 13—Mike Krzyzewski, college basketball coach

February 18—Dennis DeYoung, keyboardist and singer, Styx ("Lady")

February 24—Edward James Olmos, actor *(Battlestar Galactica)*

March 6—Rob Reiner, actor and director *(When Harry Met Sally)*

March 8—Carole Bayer Sager, songwriter ("That's What Friends Are For")

March 10—Tom Scholz, musician, Boston ("More Than a Feeling")

March 12—Mitt Romney, governor of Massachusetts

March 19—Glenn Close, actress *(Fatal Attraction)*

March 22—James Patterson, thriller writer (Along Came a Spider)

March 25—Elton John, English rock singer, songwriter, and pianist ("Rocket Man")

April 2—Emmylou Harris, country singer ("Two More Bottles of Wine")

April 6—John Ratzenberger, actor *(Cheers)*

April 8—Tom DeLay, politician

April 12—Tom Clancy, author *(The Hunt For Red October)*

April 12—David Letterman, talk show host

April 16—Kareem Abdul-Jabbar, basketball player

April 16—Gerry Rafferty, Scottish singer and songwriter ("Baker Street")

April 18—James Woods, actor *(Casino)*

April 19—Mark Volman, pop singer, the Turtles ("Happy Together")

April 21—Iggy Pop, rock singer ("Lust For Life")

April 26—Donna de Varona, 1964 Olympic gold medalist swimmer, sportscaster, and women's sports activist

April 29—Tommy James, rock singer, with the Shondells ("Mony Mony")

May 3—Doug Henning, magician

May 13—Stephen R. Donaldson, sci-fi and fantasy author (the Thomas Covenant series)

Future actress Glenn Close is born on March 19 in Greenwich, Connecticut.

May 16—Bob Edwards, radio journalist

May 29—Anthony Geary, actor *(General Hospital)*

June 1—Ronnie Wood, English rock musician, The Rolling Stones

June 6—Robert Englund, actor *(A Nightmare on Elm Street)*

June 7—Thurman Munson, baseball catcher

June 8—Sara Paretsky, crime novelist *(Deadlock)*

June 19—Salman Rushdie, Indian-born British author *(The Satanic Verses)*

June 20—Dolores "LaLa" Brooks, singer, The Crystals ("Then He Kissed Me")

June 21—Meredith Baxter, actress *(Family Ties)*

June 21—Michael Gross, actor *(Family Ties)*

June 22—"Pistol" Pete Maravich, basketball player

June 22—David L. Lander, Squiggy on *Laverne & Shirley*

June 22—Howard Kaylan, lead singer, The Turtles ("Happy Together")

June 24—Mick Fleetwood, drummer, Fleetwood Mac ("Go Your Own Way")

June 25—Jimmie Walker, comedian and actor *(Good Times)*

June 29—Richard Lewis, actor, comedian

July 2—Larry David, actor, writer *(Curb Your Enthusiasm)*

July 3—Dave Barry, humorist

July 9—Mitch Mitchell, English rock drummer, The Jimi Hendrix Experience

July 10—Arlo Guthrie, folk singer ("The City of New Orleans")

July 17—Camilla Parker-Bowles, Duchess of Cornwall, second wife of Prince Charles

July 19—Bernie Leadon, musician and songwriter, the Eagles ("Take It Easy")

July 19—Brian May, English rock guitarist, Queen ("We Will Rock You")

July 20—Carlos Santana, Mexican-born rock guitarist, Santana ("Black Magic Woman")

July 22—Albert Brooks, actor, comedian *(Broadcast News)*

July 22—Don Henley, singer-songwriter, The Eagles ("Desperado")

July 24—Robert Hays, actor *(Airplane!)*

July 28—Sally Struthers, actress *(All in the Family)*

July 30—Arnold Schwarzenegger, Austrian-born actor, bodybuilder, and governor of California

August 8—Ken Dryden, Hockey Hall of Fame goaltender

August 10—Ian Anderson, British rock musician, Jethro Tull ("Locomotive Breath")

August 14—Danielle Steel, romance novelist

August 22—Cindy Williams, actress *(Laverne & Shirley)*

August 27—Barbara Bach, actress *(The Spy Who Loved Me)*

September 6—Jane Curtin, actress *(Saturday Night Live)*

September 8—Benjamin Orr, rock musician, The Cars ("Drive")

Arnold Schwarzenegger, who would become an actor, a bodybuilder, and the 38th governor of California, is born on July 30 in Thal, Austria.

September 14—Sam Neill, New Zealand–born actor (*Jurassic Park*)

September 21—Don Felder, musician and songwriter, The Eagles ("Hotel California")

September 21—Stephen King, horror author (*The Shining*)

September 25—Cheryl Tiegs, model

September 26—Lynn Anderson, country singer ("I Never Promised You a Rose Garden")

September 27—Marvin Lee "Meat Loaf" Aday, rock singer ("Paradise by the Dashboard Light")

September 30—Marc Bolan, English rock musician, T. Rex ("Bang a Gong")

October 1—Stephen Collins, actor (*7th Heaven*)

October 5—Brian Johnson, English rock singer, AC/DC ("Back In Black")

October 12—Chris Wallace, journalist

October 13—Sammy Hagar, rock singer ("I Can't Drive 55")

October 15—Bob Weir, rock guitarist, Grateful Dead ("Truckin'")

October 17—Michael McKean, actor (*Best in Show*)

October 22—Haley Barbour, governor of Mississippi

October 24—Kevin Kline, actor (*A Fish Called Wanda*)

October 26—Hillary Rodham Clinton, First Lady, senator, U.S. secretary of state

October 26—Jaclyn Smith, actress (*Charlie's Angels*)

October 29—Richard Dreyfuss, actor (*Close Encounters of the Third Kind*)

October 30—Timothy B. Schmit, musician, The Eagles ("I Can't Tell You Why")

November 5—Peter Noone, singer, Herman's Hermits ("I'm Into Something Good")

November 8—Minnie Riperton, R&B singer ("Lovin' You")

November 13—Joe Mantegna, actor (*Criminal Minds*)

November 14—P.J. O'Rourke, journalist and humorist

November 19—Bob Boone, baseball player and manager

November 20—Joe Walsh, rock singer and guitarist ("Life's Been Good")

November 25—John Larroquette, actor (*Night Court*)

November 30—David Mamet, playwright (*Glengarry Glen Ross*)

December 5—Jim Plunkett, football player

December 7—Johnny Bench, Hall of Fame baseball player

December 8—Gregg Allman, singer and organist, Allman Brothers Band ("Melissa")

December 11—Teri Garr, actress (*Young Frankenstein*)

December 26—Carlton Fisk, Hall of Fame baseball player

December 29—Ted Danson, actor (*Cheers*)

December 30—Jeff Lynne, British rock musician, Electric Light Orchestra ("Don't Bring Me Down")

December 31—Tim Matheson, actor, film director, and producer (*Animal House*)

KAISER

KAISER-FRAZER PRODUCT

BODY STYLING

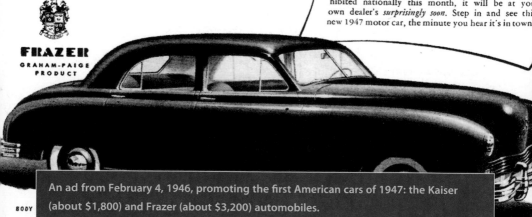

BODY

An ad from February 4, 1946, promoting the first American cars of 1947: the Kaiser (about $1,800) and Frazer (about $3,200) automobiles.

The Cost of Living in 1947

S ome economists have referred to 1947 as the start of the Great Prosperity, a period of roughly 30 years of high employment and standard of living. This flourishing period is largely credited to America's status as the world's manufacturing capital. The Great Prosperity strengthened the middle class and led to increased leisure time and consumerism. The automobile industry, always a bellwether of the American economy, was booming, with sales at an all-time high to that point.

The inflation rate for much of 1947 was very high. Indeed, the average rate for the year, 14.65%, was the fifth highest on record. But by the end of the year, it had dropped from a high of 19.7% in April to 8.5%. According to the Bureau of Labor and Statistics, a dollar in 1947 is worth $10.16 in 2012.

Still, prices for food and entertainment remained low, especially by today's standards. However, electrical appliances that we take for granted today, especially television sets, were just starting to make their way into American homes and were major purchases. The following pages contain statistics about American life and the cost of living in 1947.

A letter carrier uses his key to unlock a mail collection box mounted to a telephone pole. A first-class postage stamp costs 3 cents.

Statistics about American life in 1947:

Population: 144,126,071

Year-end close of the Dow Jones Industrial Average: 181

Minimum wage: $0.40 per hour

Average wages per year: $2,500

Median family income: $3,031

Cost of a new Levitt house in Levittown, New York: $7,500

Inflation rates:

January: 18.1%

June: 18.4%

December: 8.5%, which would be the highest rate until 1975

Average for the year: 14.65%, the fifth highest on record

Food:

Cost of a loaf of bread: $0.13, the equivalent of $1.32 in 2012 dollars

Pound of coffee: $0.55, compared to $9.99 in 2012

Dozen eggs: $0.25

Bottle of Coca-Cola: $0.05

13-oz. box of Kellogg's Corn Flakes: $0.17

Gallon of milk: $0.80, the equivalent of $8.13 in 2012 dollars

1-oz. Hershey bar: $0.05

Pork loin roast: $0.45/pound

Leg of lamb: $0.59/pound

Products:

A pair of nylons: $0.20

100-count aspirin: $0.76

First-class postage stamp: $0.03

Sealy mattress: $38

Bulova watch: $52.50

Daily issue of the *New York Times:* $0.03

Issue of the weekly *Saturday Evening Post:* $0.10, raised to $0.15 on November 15, 1947

Issue of the weekly *Life* magazine: $0.15

Men's sweater: $8.50

Men's suit: $24.50

Pack of cigarettes: $0.18

Ounce of gold: $34.71, compared with $1,771.36 in 2012

Not just once, but from 16 diffe positions, we drop sample phones from desk-top height a hardwood surface.

This machine spins dials 40 times a day — day after day — make them prove they're good at least 500,000 twirls.

We expected this . . .

YOUR TELEPHONE must take hard knocks as they come — and go on working.

To make sure it can, we test samples of each day's production and put telephones through the equivalent of years of service in a few hours or days. For example: we drop handsets into their cradles 22,000 times — equal to 4 years' normal use. We even check their feet to be certain they won't scratch your table.

Here at Western Electric, we've been making

Bell telephones since 1882. But telephones themselves are only about 6% of the equipment used in your service. The other 94% includes wire, cable, switchboards, trucks, poles, tools, office equipment. With the exception of buildings, we make or supply almost everything Bell telephone people use — and test it with utmost care.

Guarding the quality of things used in your Bell telephone service is one way that Western Electric helps to make it the world's best.

MANUFACTURER
of telephone apparatus for the Bell System.

PURCHASER
of supplies for Bell telephone companies

DISTRIBUTOR
of Bell telephone apparatus and supplies.

INSTALLER
of Bell System central office equipment.

Western Electric

A UNIT OF THE BELL SYSTEM SINCE

Western Bell's Model 302 rotary telephone can be purchased in black, ivory, bronze, silver, gold, rose, blue, green, and red.

Appliances:

Gas range: $200, the equivalent of $2,032 in 2012 dollars

10" Emerson television: $375, more than 10% of a household's average annual income

Philco refrigerator: $239

Emerson radio: $19.65, the equivalent of $199.73 in 2012 dollars

Automobiles:

Number of new passenger cars built: 3,519,900, a 55% increase over 1946

Number of new trucks built: 1,221,000, a 33% increase over 1946

Cost of a gallon of gas: $0.23, the equivalent of $2.34 in 2012 dollars

Average cost of a new car: $1,834, compared to over $30,000 in 2011

Buick Roadmaster Convertible: $2,651

Ford Deluxe coupe: $1,076

Ford Deluxe sedan: $1,130

Ford station wagon: 1,525

Ford Sportsman: $1,931

Frazer Nash standard sedan: $2,295

Hudson Commodore 6: $1,895

Oldsmobile station wagon: $2,456

Plymouth P15 Club coupe: $1,445

Studebaker M-5 Coupe Express: $1,082

Sports and entertainment:

Average movie ticket price: $0.36, compared to $7.89 in 2010

Average ticket price for a Major League Baseball game: $1.40

Average salary of a Major League Baseball player: $11,300

Salary of American League Most Valuable Player Joe DiMaggio: $43,750

In the spring of 1947, singers Kitty Kallen and Doris Day are photographed for the cover of *Down Beat* magazine. Day's breakthrough came two years previously, with the song "Sentimental Journey"; her movie career would not take off for another few years.

Day-by-Day Calendar of
1947

By 1947, much of Europe was struggling to recover from the devastation of World War II. This instability led to unrest in Italy, Poland, and several other countries. The creation of the Communist Bloc empowered the Soviets, who looked to expand their empire across Europe. In addition, the Nazi leaders who had been captured were beginning to be placed on trial for their atrocities.

In response, President Truman created the Marshall Plan, which offered financial assistance to any European nation, and the Truman Doctrine, which provided military aid to Greece and Turkey to prevent a Soviet takeover. The ensuing increase in tension between the United States and the Soviets, a tension not accompanied by bloodshed, was the start of the Cold War.

But the turmoil in 1947 was not confined to Europe. The Indian subcontinent continued its decades-long struggle for independence from Great Britain, which resulted in the creation of India and Pakistan in August. Almost immediately, the two new nations went to war for control over the territories of Jammu and Kashmir. The British government allowed the United Nations to determine the future of Palestine, which led to many outbreaks of violence between Jews and Arabs.

However, the United States enjoyed a period of comparative tranquility thanks to the economic boom. The growth of the suburbs was beginning with the birth of Levittown, New York, and the struggle for civil rights for African Americans began to pick up steam. But Americans mostly spent their increased leisure time on enjoyable pursuits—listening to the radio, going to movies, and attending sporting events.

JANUARY 1

The University of Illinois Fighting Illini defeats the UCLA Bruins, 45–14, in the 33rd Rose Bowl in Pasadena, California.

JANUARY 2

Mahatma Gandhi begins a march in East Bengal for peace.

JANUARY 3

The 80th Congress opens in Washington, D.C.

JANUARY 4

The U.S. Senate appoints Rev. Peter Marshall of the New York Avenue Presbyterian Church as its chaplain.

JANUARY 5

Humphrey Bogart and Lauren Bacall appear on comedian Jack Benny's weekly radio show.

JANUARY 6

President Truman delivers his State of the Union address, the first to be televised.

JANUARY 7

It's a Wonderful Life goes into general release in theaters across the United States after a nearly three-week run at the Globe Theater in New York City.

JANUARY 8

Don Dendell, author of historical novels, is born in Akron, Ohio.

JANUARY 9

Elizabeth Short, the "Black Dahlia," was last seen alive by the bell captain of the Biltmore Hotel in Los Angeles.

JANUARY 10

Finian's Rainbow opens on Broadway at the 46th Street Theatre and runs for 725 performances.

JANUARY 17

News of the brutal murder of the "Black Dahlia" spreads across the country as police continue their investigation.

JANUARY 18

"The Old Lamp-Lighter" by Sammy Kaye begins its fourth week atop *Billboard*'s "Best Sellers in Stores" chart.

JANUARY 19

Fraudulent elections in Poland give almost total control of the national legislature to the Communists.

JANUARY 20

Josh Gibson, a Negro Leagues baseball player known as the "black Babe Ruth," dies at the age of 35.

JANUARY 21

Mickey Cochrane, Frank Frisch, Lefty Grove, and Carl Hubbell are elected to the Baseball Hall of Fame.

JANUARY 22

KTLA, the first commercial television station in Los Angeles, begins broadcasting, with Bob Hope hosting "the Western Premiere of Commercial Television."

JANUARY 23

President Truman holds a press conference in his office in the White House.

JANUARY 24

The National Football League adds a fifth official, called a back judge, to watch the defensive backs, and allows sudden-death overtime to break ties in playoff games.

JANUARY 25

Al Capone, notorious Chicago gangster, dies in his home in Florida at the age of 48.

JANUARY 26

Opera soprano Grace Moore and Prince Gustaf Adolf of Sweden are among those killed in a plane crash in Copenhagen, Denmark.

JANUARY 27

Vallabhbhai Patel, a leader in India's struggle for independence, appears on the cover of *Time* magazine.

JANUARY 28

A blizzard hits Milwaukee, Wisconsin, dumping 18 inches of snow on the Midwestern city over a three-day period.

JANUARY 29

Bob Hope and Dorothy Lamour appear on *Philco Radio Time,* hosted by their costar in the "Road" film series, Bing Crosby.

JANUARY 30

Steve Marriott, guitarist and singer with the Small Faces ("Itchykoo Park") and Humble Pie ("Natural Born Bugie"), is born in London.

JANUARY 31

The USS *South Dakota,* which deployed for two tours in the Pacific theater during World War II, is decommissioned.

FEBRUARY 1

A matinee performance of Charles Gounod's *Romeo et Juliette,* an operatic version of Shakespeare's play, is broadcast on the radio from the Metropolitan Opera in New York. The performance stars Jussi Björling and Bidú Sayão.

FEBRUARY 2

I'll Be Yours, a musical comedy starring Deanna Durbin, William Bendix, and Adolphe Menjou, opens in movie theaters nationwide.

Ernest Tubb's "Rainbow at Midnight" is a no. 1 hit, as certified by *Billboard* magazine.

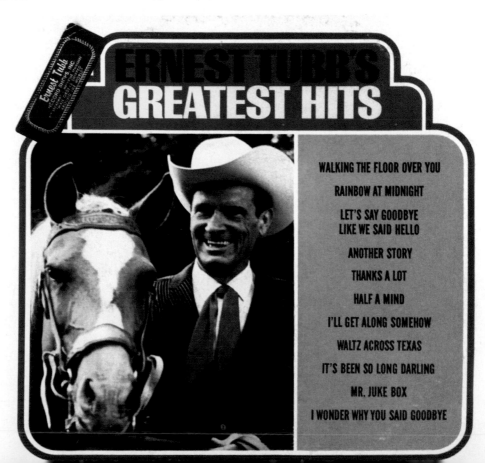

FEBRUARY 3

The lowest recorded temperature in North American history, −81.4°F, is reached in Snag, Yukon Territory, Canada.

FEBRUARY 4

One year from today, Ceylon (now Sri Lanka) would gain its independence from the United Kingdom.

FEBRUARY 5

Astronaut Mary Cleave, who would fly on two space shuttle missions, is born in Southampton, NY.

FEBRUARY 6

The Basketball Association of America (BAA), the forerunner of the National Basketball Association, progresses through its inaugural season.

FEBRUARY 7

Wayne Allwine, the voice of Mickey Mouse in films and TV specials for 32 years, is born in Glendale, CA.

FEBRUARY 8

KSD-TV in St. Louis begins broadcasting. At the time,
only four televisions were in use in the St. Louis area.

FEBRUARY 9

Soul singer Major Harris, who had a top five hit in 1975 with
"Love Won't Let Me Wait," is born in Richmond, Virginia.

FEBRUARY 10

Actress Deborah Kerr, star of *Black Narcissus,*
appears on the cover of *Time* magazine.

FEBRUARY 11

The Shocking Miss Pilgrim opens in theaters nationwide. The film is the
debut of Marilyn Monroe, who appears onscreen for a few seconds.

FEBRUARY 12

In Paris, fashion designer Christian Dior launches his
first collection, which is later dubbed "the New Look."

FEBRUARY 13

Oil is discovered near Leduc, Alberta, Canada, sparking
a boom in the oil industry across Western Canada.

FEBRUARY 14

The British government announces that it will allow the
United Nations to determine the future of Palestine.

FEBRUARY 15

"(I Love You) For Sentimental Reasons" by the King Cole Trio,
led by Nat "King" Cole on piano and vocals, begins its
first week atop *Billboard*'s "Best Sellers in Stores" chart.

FEBRUARY 16

All six teams in the National Hockey League are in action.

FEBRUARY 17

Voice of America, the international radio broadcasting
arm of the U.S. government, begins sending
Russian-language broadcasts into the Soviet Union.

FEBRUARY 18

The *Red Arrow*, a train bound for New York from Detroit, derails near Altoona, Pennsylvania, killing 24 people.

Gangster Al Capone (b. 1899) dies in his home on January 25.

FEBRUARY 19

President Truman asks Congress to repeal emergency and wartime powers granted to the presidency during World War II.

FEBRUARY 20

An explosion at the O'Conner Electro-Plating Corporation in downtown Los Angeles kills 15.

FEBRUARY 21

Edwin Land introduces the first instant camera, the Polaroid Land, at a meeting of the Optical Society of America in New York.

FEBRUARY 22

"Open the Door, Richard" by Count Basie spends the week at number one on *Billboard*'s "Best Sellers in Stores" chart.

FEBRUARY 23

John J. McCloy is elected the second president of the World Bank.

FEBRUARY 24

King George II of Greece appears on the cover of *Time* magazine.

FEBRUARY 25

The last remnant of the state of Prussia is officially abolished and dissolved into Germany.

FEBRUARY 26

Jazz saxophonist Charlie Parker records four songs with his New Stars group in Los Angeles.

FEBRUARY 27

In Taiwan, a cigarette vendor's arrest leads to protests against the corruption and repression of the Chinese government.

FEBRUARY 28

Protests in Taiwan from the night before devolve into riots in what came to be known as the 228 Incident.

MARCH 1

The International Monetary Fund begins operations.

MARCH 2

Teachers in Buffalo, New York, end a one-week strike when Mayor Bernard J. Dowd agrees to raise their salaries between $300 and $625.

MARCH 3

Singer Jennifer Warnes ("Up Where We Belong," "(I've Had) The Time of My Life,") is born in Seattle.

MARCH 4

The Two Mrs. Carrolls, starring Humphrey Bogart and Barbara Stanwyck, opens in movie theaters across America.

MARCH 5

Relief pitcher Kent Tekulve, who would spend 16 years in the major leagues, is born in Cincinnati, Ohio.

MARCH 6

The Chinese army is sent to Taiwan to stop the riots,
resulting in the slaughter of thousands of citizens.

MARCH 7

President Truman signs proclamation declaring April 6 to
be Army Day, with April 6–12 to be declared Army Week.

A commemorative "first day cover" marks 100 years since the
Postal Service adopted the adhesive postage stamp.

MARCH 8

"Managua, Nicaragua" by Freddy Martin begins its second week atop the *Billboard* "Best Sellers in Stores" chart.

MARCH 9

Carrie Chapman Catt, one of the leaders in the women's suffrage movement, dies in New Rochelle, New York, at the age of 88.

MARCH 10

General of the army George C. Marshall, who was appointed secretary of state on January 21, 1947, appears on the cover of *Time* magazine.

MARCH 11

President Truman writes to former president Herbert Hoover thanking him for his advice on how to deal with the food shortages in Germany and Austria.

MARCH 12

President Truman announces the Truman Doctrine, which gives economic and military aid to Greece and Turkey to help stop the spread of Communism. This date is seen as the start of the Cold War.

MARCH 13

The 19th Academy Awards are held in Los Angeles. *The Best Years of Our Lives* wins seven awards, including Best Picture.

MARCH 14

A treaty is signed between the United States and the Philippines for the establishment of American military bases in the Philippines.

MARCH 15

"Heartaches" by Ted Weems begins a 12-week run at number one on *Billboard*'s "Best Sellers in Stores" chart.

MARCH 16

The Red House, a psychological thriller starring Edward G. Robinson and Julie London, opens in movie theaters.

MARCH 17

The North American B-45 Tornado, the Air Force's first operational jet bomber, has its first flight.

MARCH 18

The Federal Communications Commission denies a
request by the Columbia Broadcasting System to begin
broadcasting commercial television shows in color.

MARCH 19

Danny Kaye and Peggy Lee appear on *Philco Radio Time,* hosted by Bing Crosby.

MARCH 20

Holy Cross defeats Navy, 55–47, in their opening
match of the NCAA basketball tournament.

MARCH 21

The 22nd amendment to the Constitution, which imposes
a two-term limit on presidents, is passed by Congress.
It would be ratified by the states on February 27, 1951.

MARCH 22

President Truman issues an executive order setting
up a program empowering the Justice Department to
conduct loyalty investigations among federal employees.

MARCH 23

The National Hockey League concludes its regular season.

A promotional brochure for listeners of NBC Radio's Chesterfield Supper Club in 1947, sponsored by Chesterfield Cigarettes.

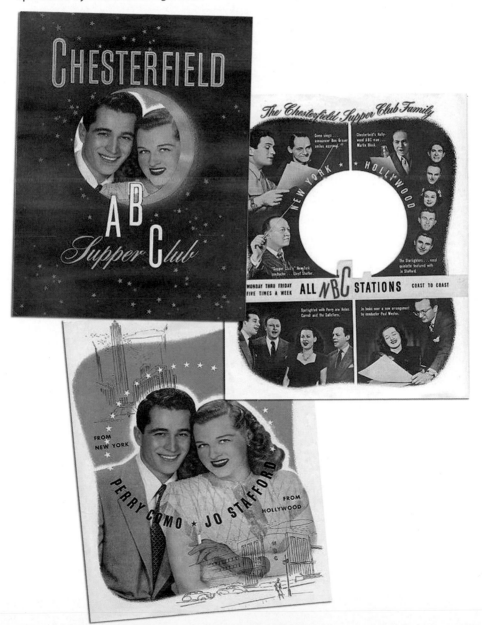

MARCH 24

John D. Rockefeller Jr. donates a 17-acre tract of land along New York's East River to serve as the home of the United Nations.

MARCH 25

Holy Cross wins the NCAA basketball championship, defeating Oklahoma 58–47, at Madison Square Garden in New York.

MARCH 26

President Truman holds his 100th news conference as president in his office in the White House.

MARCH 27

Bob Hope and Groucho Marx appear in a 10-minute sketch on radio's *Walgreen Hour*.

MARCH 28

Baseball fans across the country get ready for the new season as spring training begins to wind down.

MARCH 29

A revolt against French colonial rule begins on
the island of Madagascar off the coast of Africa.

MARCH 30

An episode of the radio show *The Bickersons,*
"John's New Fishing Pole," is broadcast on CBS.

MARCH 31

The Basketball Association of America concludes its first regular season
with the Chicago Stags defeating the St. Louis Bombers in overtime, 73–66.

APRIL 1

King George II of Greece dies at his palace in Athens.

APRIL 2

The Convair XB-46, an experimental bomber that was
canceled before completing its test phase, has its first flight.

APRIL 9

A series of tornadoes strikes a 220-mile path through
Texas, Oklahoma, and Kansas, killing 181 people.

APRIL 10

The Journey of Reconciliation, in which 16 white and black members
of the Congress on Racial Equality rode buses through the South
for two weeks to test anti-segregation laws, enters its second day.

APRIL 11

The Buchenwald trial, in which 31 members of the staff of the
Buchenwald concentration camp would be found guilty of war
crimes, begins at the former Dachau concentration camp in Germany.

APRIL 12

"Birth of a Notion," a Warner Brothers cartoon short
starring Mel Blanc as Daffy Duck, is released.

APRIL 13

Four participants in the Journey of Reconciliation, two white and two
black. are arrested in Greensboro, North Carolina, for their participation.

APRIL 14

Charles de Gaulle founds the Rally of the
French People Party in Strasbourg, France.

APRIL 15

Jackie Robinson becomes the first African
American to play in Major League Baseball.

APRIL 16

The worst industrial disaster in American history takes place
when the SS *Grandcamp* explodes in Port of Texas City, Texas.

APRIL 17

The Journey of Reconciliation reaches Knoxville and
Nashville, Tennessee, where its participants hold meetings
and give lectures on the importance of nonviolence.

APRIL 18

All of the fires caused by the Texas City Disaster are extinguished
after three days. Nearly 600 people were killed as a result
of the explosion, which also caused $600 million in damage.

APRIL 19

The Toronto Maple Leafs win the Stanley Cup, defeating
the Montreal Canadiens in game six of the finals.

APRIL 20

Frederick IX becomes king of Denmark following the death of Christian X.

APRIL 21

William A. Patterson, president of United Airlines,
appears on the cover of *Time* magazine.

APRIL 22

The Philadelphia Warriors defeat the Chicago Stags, 83–80, in game
six of the BAA finals to win the league's first championship.

APRIL 23

The Journey of Reconciliation ends in Washington, D.C.

APRIL 24

Willa Cather, author of *My Ántonia* and *One of Ours,* dies at 73.

The April 6 Army Day Parade on Market Street in San Francisco, California.

APRIL 25

President Truman opens the first bowling alley in the White House.

APRIL 26

Junkyard Garden by John Atherton is on the cover of the *Saturday Evening Post.*

APRIL 27

The New York Yankees honor their legendary slugger with "Babe Ruth Day" at Yankee Stadium.

APRIL 28

Norwegian writer Thor Heyerdahl begins his journey from South America to Polynesia in the *Kon-Tiki,* a ship made out of balsa wood.

APRIL 29

The official report on the causes and events of the Texas City Disaster is produced by the Fire Prevention and Engineering Bureau of Texas and the National Board of Fire Underwriters.

APRIL 30

Boulder Dam is renamed the Hoover Dam.

MAY 1

The Cleveland Indians make Cleveland Municipal Stadium their home, which it would remain until 1993. Before this they had split their home games between Municipal Stadium and League Park.

MAY 2

The Christmas classic movie *Miracle on 34th Street* opens in theaters.

MAY 3

Norman Rockwell's *Merry-Go-Round* appears
on the cover of the *Saturday Evening Post*.

MAY 4

The Irgun, a underground paramilitary Zionist organization, breaks into Acre Prison in Palestine, freeing 28 Jewish political prisoners.

MAY 5

Palmiro Tagliotti, leader of the Italian Communist
Party, appears on the cover of *Time* magazine.

MAY 6

A brief earthquake hits a large section of southeastern Wisconsin near Milwaukee.

MAY 7

Real estate developer William Levitt announces plans to build 2,000
rental homes for returning veterans in a section of Long Island, New York,
called Island Trees. The area would eventually be renamed Levittown.

MAY 8

Family Theater, a dramatic anthology radio show on the Mutual
Broadcasting Network, broadcasts an episode called "The Awakening."

MAY 9

The World Bank makes its first loan, giving $250 million to France.

MAY 10

Duke Ellington and His Orchestra performs six
songs at WNEW Radio Studios in New York.

MAY 11

The B.F. Goodrich Company announces the development of a tubeless
tire, which would make automobiles safer and more efficient.

Henry Ford's auto company would last many decades after his death on April 7. Early-model
Ford cars, like this restored Model T, would become collector treasures.

MAY 12

Senator Arthur Vandeberg, chairman of the Senate Foreign
Relations Committee, appears on the cover of *Time* magazine.

MAY 13

The Senate votes 68–21 to pass a bill introduced by Robert
Taft that weakens the power of labor unions. The House passed
a similar bill, introduced by Fred Hartley, a month earlier.

MAY 14

The Other Love, starring Barbara Stanwyck
and David Niven, opens in movie theaters.

MAY 15

President Truman holds a news conference in his office in the White House.

MAY 16

A game between the New York Yankees and the Boston
Red Sox at Yankee Stadium is attended by 74,747 fans,
then the largest crowd to ever see a baseball game.

MAY 17

Seabiscuit, champion thoroughbred racehorse
and subject of a 2003 movie, dies at 13.

MAY 18

Radio station WLIP begins broadcasting in Kenosha, Wisconsin.

MAY 19

J. Arthur Rank, British industrialist and producer of such
films as *Black Narcissus, A Matter of Life and Death,* and
The Jake's Progress, appears on the cover of *Time* magazine.

MAY 20

A total solar eclipse, the first since 1945, takes place.

MAY 21

A Greenville, South Carolina, jury acquits 31 white people of
lynching Willie Earle, a black man accused of stabbing a white
cab driver, despite having confessions from 26 of the defendants.

MAY 28

Jazz singer Billie Holiday pleads guilty to charges of narcotics possession and begins an eight-month prison sentence in Alderson, West Virginia.

MAY 29

A United Airlines flight from New York to Cleveland overruns the runway at LaGuardia Airport and crashes into an embankment, killing 43 of the 48 people on board.

MAY 30

Hungarian prime minister Ferenc Nagy is forced to resign and sent into exile following the kidnapping of his son by Soviet-backed Communists.

MAY 31

"Heartaches," by Ted Weems, ends its 12-week run at number one on *Billboard*'s "Best Sellers in Stores" chart.

JUNE 1

A tornado near Pine Bluff, Arkansas, kills more than 30 people.

JUNE 2

Broadway producer Billy Rose, who wrote the lyrics for
such standards as "Me and My Shadow" and "It's Only a
Paper Moon," is featured on the cover of *Time* magazine.

JUNE 3

The British government proposes a plan to
grant independence to India and Pakistan.

JUNE 4

The House of Representatives passes the Taft-Hartley Act.

JUNE 5

Secretary of state George Marshall establishes the Marshall Plan
to help rebuild Europe following the devastation of World War II.

JUNE 6

The Boston Pops, conducted by Arthur Fiedler, performs Leroy Anderson's
Irish Suite, a piece commissioned by the Eire Society of Boston.

JUNE 13

The Mutual Radio Network broadcasts
episode 23 in its *Superman vs. Kryptonite* series.

JUNE 14

"Dr. Jekyll and Mr. Mouse," the 30th
Tom and Jerry animated short, is released.

JUNE 15

The United Nations Special Committee on Palestine (UNSCOP)
arrives in Palestine and holds hearings with Zionist organizations.
The Arab Higher Committee refuses to meet with UNSCOP.

JUNE 16

Ernest Gruening, governor of the Alaska Territory and advocate
for Alaskan statehood, is featured on the cover of *Time* magazine.

JUNE 17

Pan Am becomes the first airline to have
regularly scheduled around-the-world flights.

JUNE 18

Ewell Blackwell of the Cincinnati Reds pitches
a no-hitter against the Boston Braves.

JUNE 19

British and French foreign ministers contact 22 European nations to
arrange a meeting in Paris to deal with European economic recovery.

JUNE 20

Bugsy Siegel, the gangster who helped build
Las Vegas, is killed in his Beverly Hills home.

JUNE 21

"Peg o' My Heart" by the Harmonicats is the number
one song on *Billboard*'s "Best Sellers in Stores" chart.

JUNE 22

A world record is set when 12 inches of rain
fall on Holt, Missouri, in only 42 minutes.

JUNE 29

President Truman becomes the first president
to give an address before the NAACP.

JUNE 30

Mohandas K. Gandhi appears on the cover of *Time* magazine.

JULY 1

The BAA holds its first amateur draft in Detroit, Michigan. With the first pick, the
Pittsburgh Ironmen select Clifton McNeely of Texas Wesleyan University.

JULY 2

The Soviet Union rejects the United States' offer
of economic aid under the Marshall Plan.

JULY 3

Cleveland Indians owner Bill Veeck purchases the contract
of Larry Doby from the Newark Eagles of the Negro League.

JULY 4

President Truman gives an Independence Day address
at Monticello, the home of Thomas Jefferson.

JULY 5

Larry Doby becomes Major League Baseball's second
African-American player, and the first black player in the American
League, when he makes his debut for the Cleveland Indians.

JULY 6

The AK-47 assault rifle goes into production in the Soviet Union.

JULY 7

William Brazel contacts Roswell, New Mexico, sheriff George Wilcox
about some unusual debris he found on a ranch where he worked.
This is the beginning of the famous Roswell UFO Incident, which
would help spark a decades-long discussion about extraterrestrial life.

JULY 8

The American League defeats the National League, 2–1, in the 14th
All-Star Game. The contest is played at Wrigley Field in Chicago.

JULY 9

Lt. Col. Florence Blanchfield, superintendent of the Army
Nurse Corps, becomes the first woman to be named an
officer in the U.S. Army. She is appointed by Gen. Eisenhower.

JULY 10

Princess Elizabeth of England announces her
engagement to Lieutenant Philip Mountbatten.

JULY 11

The SS *Exodus* departs France for Palestine with
over 4,500 Jewish passengers, many of whom were
Holocaust survivors and traveling without legal paperwork.

JULY 12

The Conference of European Economic Cooperation, which
brings together representatives from all the countries
accepting aid under the Marshall Plan, begins in Paris.

JULY 13

Baseball fans all over America enjoy this Sunday afternoon,
as 14 of the 16 teams play in doubleheaders.

JULY 14

Elizabeth Taylor, star of *Life With Father,* is
featured on the cover of *Life* magazine.

JULY 15

Gunfighters, a Western starring Randolph Scott and
Forrest Tucker, opens in movie theaters nationwide.

In July, the first full commissioned officer class of dietetic interns graduates at the
U.S. Public Health Service Hospital, Staten Island, New York.

JULY 16

Boxer Rocky Graziano wins the middleweight title in
Chicago after knocking out Tony Zale in the sixth round.

JULY 17

Raoul Wallenberg, a Swedish businessman who rescued tens
of thousands of Jews during the Holocaust, is reported to have
died under mysterious circumstances while in a Soviet prison.

JULY 18

The SS *Exodus* is boarded on the Mediterranean Sea near Haifa,
Palestine, by British troops, who take over the ship and
subsequently demand that the ship be returned to France.
Two passengers and one crew member die in the skirmish.

JULY 19

Prime minister Aung San and eight leaders of Burma's pre-independence interim
government are killed by their political rivals during a meeting in Rangoon.

JULY 20

Jewish passengers are ordered off the *Exodus* in Haifa
and placed on other ships for deportation back to Europe.

JULY 21

George A. Smith, president of the Church of Jesus Christ of Latter-Day Saints, appears on the cover of *Time* magazine.

JULY 22

Crossfire, a crime thriller starring Robert Young and Robert Mitchum, opens in theaters.

JULY 23

AMVETS becomes the first World War II organization to be chartered by Congress.

JULY 24

President Truman holds a news conference in his office in the White House.

JULY 25

President Truman meets with Gen. Dwight Eisenhower to discuss the appointment of the first secretary of defense.

AUGUST 2

The SS *Exodus* arrives at Port-de-Bouc, near Marseilles, France.

AUGUST 3

Opera fans read about the successful Italian debut of soprano Maria Callas in Ponchielli's *La Giaconda* the night before.

AUGUST 4

David E. Lilienthal, chairman of the U.S. Atomic Energy Commission, is featured on the cover of *Time* magazine.

AUGUST 5

Guitarist Rick Derringer, who would have a number one hit in 1965 with "Hang on Sloopy" as a member of the McCoys, as well as a popular solo career, is born in Ohio.

AUGUST 6

Howard Hughes testifies before the Senate War Investigating Committee concerning allegations of corruption into his receipt of government contracts.

AUGUST 7

Thor Heyerdahl smashes the *Kon-Tiki* into a reef at Raroia in the Tuamotu Islands after a 101-day journey of more than 4,300 miles across the Pacific Ocean.

AUGUST 8

President Truman publicly announces the judges who will preside over the upcoming Nuremberg trials.

AUGUST 9

"Smoke! Smoke! Smoke! (That Cigarette)" by Tex Williams begins a six-week run atop *Billboard*'s "Best Sellers in Stores" chart.

AUGUST 10

Pilot William Odom sets a world record for a solo around-the-world flight, going from Chicago to Chicago in 73 hours and five minutes.

AUGUST 11

Actress Ella Raines *(Phantom Lady)* appears on the cover of *Life* magazine.

AUGUST 18

The Hewlett-Packard Company is incorporated.

AUGUST 19

Judges at the Nuremberg trials set a code to determine the ethics of medical research on humans in subsequent war crimes trials.

AUGUST 20

Navy Cmdr. Turner F. Caldwell sets a world air-speed record of 640.6 miles per hour in a Douglas D-558-1 Skystreak.

AUGUST 21

The first parking meters in San Francisco are installed.

AUGUST 22

Nat "King" Cole records "Nature Boy" and four other songs at Radio Recorders in Los Angeles.

AUGUST 23

President Truman's daughter Margaret makes her outdoor singing debut at the Hollywood Bowl.

AUGUST 24

Novelist Paulo Coelho is born in Rio de Janeiro.

AUGUST 25

The UN Security Council passes a resolution to offer assistance in settling the Indonesian national revolution peacefully.

AUGUST 26

NBC Radio broadcasts "A Salute to the Railroads," an episode of the *Milton Berle Show*.

AUGUST 27

The IG Farben trial, which accused directors of the German chemical conglomerate of Nazi war crimes, begins in Nuremberg, Germany.

SEPTEMBER 3

The NBC Radio Network broadcasts the "Dennis Runs for Mayor" episode of *A Day in the Life of Dennis Day*.

SEPTEMBER 4

A tropical storm develops off the French West African coast and begins to head west across the Atlantic Ocean.

SEPTEMBER 5

Humphrey Bogart and Lauren Bacall's thriller *Dark Passage* premieres in movie theaters.

SEPTEMBER 6

After the Movie by Stevan Dohanos appears on the cover of the *Saturday Evening Post*.

SEPTEMBER 7

The Baltimore Colts play their first-ever game, a 16–7 victory over the Brooklyn Dodgers of the All-America Football Conference.

SEPTEMBER 8

Author C.S. Lewis appears on the cover of *Time* magazine.

SEPTEMBER 9

During the testing of the Mark II computer at Harvard University,
a moth gets trapped in a relay, causing a malfunction.
The term "bug" is coined to describe any glitch in software.

SEPTEMBER 10

The tropical storm moving across the Atlantic is classified as a hurricane.

SEPTEMBER 11

Ralph Kiner of the Pittsburgh Pirates hits three
home runs in a game against the Boston Braves.

SEPTEMBER 12

Walt Disney Productions releases "Wide Open
Spaces," an animated short starring Donald Duck.

SEPTEMBER 19

The hurricane that hit Fort Lauderdale two days earlier reaches New Orleans with sustained winds of 96 mph.

SEPTEMBER 20

"Near You" by Francis Craig begins its 12-week run at number one on *Billboard*'s "Best Sellers in Stores" chart.

SEPTEMBER 21

The Fort Lauderdale hurricane dissolves over southern Missouri, but not before killing 51 people and doing $110 million in damage across the South.

SEPTEMBER 22

Jackie Robinson appears on the cover of *Time* magazine.

SEPTEMBER 23

A law in Argentina that gives women the right to vote is passed, largely due to the work of First Lady Eva Peron.

SEPTEMBER 24

The Foxes of Harrow, starring Rex Harrison
and Maureen O'Hara, opens in theaters.

SEPTEMBER 25

Railroaded!, a *film noir* movie starring John Ireland, Sheila Ryan,
and Hugh Beaumont, opens in theaters nationwide.

SEPTEMBER 26

Hugh Lofting, creator of the Doctor Doolittle
series of books, dies in California at age 61.

SEPTEMBER 27

Apple Picking Time, a painting by John Falter,
appears on the cover of the *Saturday Evening Post.*

SEPTEMBER 28

The Adventures of Sherlock Holmes moves to the Mutual
Broadcasting Network and opens its 13th season
with "The Case of the Dog Who Changed Its Mind."

OCTOBER 5

President Harry Truman makes the first televised
presidential address from the White House.

OCTOBER 6

The Yankees beat the Dodgers in game seven of the
1947 World Series for their 11th world championship.

OCTOBER 7

Magic Town, a romantic comedy starring James Stewart
and Jane Wyman, opens in theaters across America.

OCTOBER 8

The United States Strategic Bombing Survey, a committee designed
to study the effectiveness of Allied aerial campaigns in World War II,
is abolished following the completion of its three-year mission.

OCTOBER 9

President Truman holds a news conference in his office at the White House.

OCTOBER 10

Unconquered, a Cecil B. DeMille Western starring Gary Cooper and Paulette Goddard, opens in movie theaters.

OCTOBER 11

Norman Rockwell's *Flirting Soda Jerk* appears on the cover of the *Saturday Evening Post.*

OCTOBER 12

The second episode of NBC's *Ford Theatre* radio show is an adaptation of the 1940 Preston Sturges movie comedy *The Great McGinty.*

OCTOBER 13

William Green, president of the American Federation of Labor, appears on the cover of *Time* magazine.

OCTOBER 14

Air Force captain Chuck Yeager becomes the first person to break the sound barrier in an aircraft, reaching Mach 1.06 at Muroc Army Air Field (now Edwards Air Force Base) in California.

OCTOBER 15

The National Hockey League begins its 1947–1948 season.

OCTOBER 16

David Zucker, director of *Airplane!* and the *Naked Gun*
film series, is born in Milwaukee, Wisconsin.

OCTOBER 17

This Time for Keeps, a movie musical starring
Esther Williams and Jimmy Durante, is released.

OCTOBER 18

Bury Me Dead, a *film noir* movie starring June
Lockhart and Hugh Beaumont, opens in theaters.

OCTOBER 19

The Adventures of Sam Spade, a radio series based on Dashiell Hammett's
detective novels, broadcasts "The Untouchable Caper" on the CBS network.

OCTOBER 20

The House Un-American Activities Committee (HUAC) begins investigations into possible Communist involvement in the film industry.

OCTOBER 21

Ai Ogawa, National Book Award–winning poet,
is born Florence Anthony in Albany, Texas.

Liberty Tunnel frames the eerie sight of Pittsburgh in the midmorning smog.

OCTOBER 22

War breaks out between India and Pakistan
over the territories of Jammu and Kashmir.

OCTOBER 23

Screen Actors Guild president Ronald Reagan testifies
before HUAC about the threat of Communism in Hollywood.

OCTOBER 24

Walt Disney appears as a witness before HUAC to describe
suspected Communist involvement in a cartoonist strike in 1941.

OCTOBER 25

"Ragamuffin Ball," an episode of the radio situation comedy
The Life of Riley starring William Bendix, is broadcast on NBC.

OCTOBER 26

Maharaja Hari Singh cedes control over Jammu and Kashmir to India.

OCTOBER 27

You Bet Your Life, a radio quiz show starring
Groucho Marx, debuts on the ABC network.

OCTOBER 28

Oregon governor Earl Snell and three others are
killed in a plane crash near Dog Lake, Oregon.

OCTOBER 29

The President's Committee on Civil Rights releases a report, *To Secure
These Rights,* which calls for the end of segregation across America.

OCTOBER 30

The General Agreement on Tariffs and Trade is signed by
23 countries in Geneva, Switzerland. The agreement was
created to promote fair trade between member nations.

OCTOBER 31

Clark Clifford, special counsel to President
Truman, outlines a European recovery plan.

NOVEMBER 1

"Slick Hare," a cartoon short featuring Bugs Bunny and Elmer Fudd that parodies many Hollywood celebrities, is released.

NOVEMBER 2

The "Spruce Goose," the wooden "flying boat" with a 320-foot wingspan designed by Howard Hughes, makes its only flight.

NOVEMBER 3

University of Michigan football star Robert Chappuis appears on the cover of *Time* magazine.

NOVEMBER 4

A committee created to write a constitution for India submits its draft to the Constituent Assembly.

NOVEMBER 5

"Diathermy Machine," an episode of the radio show *The Saint*, starring Vincent Price as Simon Templar, is broadcast on CBS.

NOVEMBER 6

Meet the Press debuts on NBC.

Chuck Yeager becomes the first man to break the sound barrier, flying the experimental Bell X-1 at Mach 1 at an altitude of 45,000 feet on October 14.

NOVEMBER 7

Florida State University students vote to determine the
new nickname for their athletic teams. Two days later
the winning nickname, Seminoles, was announced.

NOVEMBER 8

Norman Rockwell's *Babysitter With Screaming Infant*
appears on the cover of the *Saturday Evening Post*.

NOVEMBER 9

The Cleveland Symphony Orchestra, conducted by George Szell, performs
Schumann's Symphony no. 4 in D Minor, "Dance of the Seven Veils"
from *Salome* by Richard Strauss, and Beethoven's Symphony
no. 7 in A Major at the Hill Auditorium in Ann Arbor, Michigan.

NOVEMBER 10

Actress Rita Hayworth, star of *Down to Earth,*
appears on the cover of *Life* magazine.

NOVEMBER 11

Gentleman's Agreement, which would win the Academy
Award for Best Picture in 1948, opens in New York.

NOVEMBER 12

The BAA begins its second season with the Washington Capitols defeating the Baltimore Bullets, 63–55.

NOVEMBER 13

Out of the Past, a thriller starring Robert Mitchum and Kirk Douglas, opens in theaters.

NOVEMBER 14

The UN passes a resolution calling for elections in Korea with the intention of uniting the nation, which had split along the 38th parallel following World War II.

NOVEMBER 15

Louis Armstrong and the All-Stars perform at Carnegie Hall in New York.

NOVEMBER 16

Actress Lana Turner *(Green Dolphin Street)* appears on an episode of the *Charlie McCarthy Show.*

NOVEMBER 17

French general and statesman Charles de Gaulle
appears on the cover of *Time* magazine.

NOVEMBER 18

Mary Kay and Johnny, the first situation comedy on network
television, debuts on the DuMont Television Network.

NOVEMBER 19

King George VI of Great Britain names Philip Mountbatten as the
Duke of Edinburgh in advance of his marriage to Princess Elizabeth.

NOVEMBER 20

Princess Elizabeth marries Philip, Duke of
Edinburgh, at Westminster Abbey, London.

NOVEMBER 21

Pianist Thelonious Monk records his "'Round Midnight"
for Blue Note records at WOR Studios in New York.

NOVEMBER 22

The 64th Harvard-Yale football game is played. Yale wins 31–21.

A number of women are posed in an office setting at the Bureau of Internal Revenue. The purpose of the photo is to document, for the National Institute for Occupational Safety and Health, the effects of improved lighting in the work environment.

NOVEMBER 23

San Francisco's KPO radio station becomes KNBC and celebrates with a broadcast featuring Harold Peary, Fred Allen, and Edgar Bergen with Charlie McCarthy.

NOVEMBER 24

The "Hollywood Ten," screenwriters who refused to testify before the House Un-American Activities Committee, are cited for being in contempt of Congress.

NOVEMBER 25

New Zealand becomes autonomous from the British Empire when its parliament passes the Statute of Westminster Adoption Act 1947.

NOVEMBER 26

Americans prepare for the next day's celebration of Thanksgiving.

NOVEMBER 27

Joe DiMaggio of the New York Yankees wins his third American League Most Valuable Player award, beating Ted Williams of the Boston Red Sox by one vote.

NOVEMBER 28

"Chip an' Dale," the third animated short starring
Walt Disney's cartoon chipmunks, is released.

NOVEMBER 29

The United Nations votes to partition the British Mandate for
Palestine, paving the way for the creation of the state of Israel.

NOVEMBER 30

Louis Armstrong and the All-Stars perform at Symphony Hall in Boston.

DECEMBER 1

Johnny Lujack is awarded the Heisman Trophy after
leading the Notre Dame Fighting Irish to a 9–0 record.

DECEMBER 2

Arabs riot in Jerusalem in protest of the UN's vote to
partition Palestine. The violence continues for three days.

DECEMBER 3

Tennessee Williams' play *A Streetcar Named Desire,* starring Marlon Brando and Jessica Tandy, opens on Broadway at the Ethel Barrymore Theater.

DECEMBER 4

Sen. Robert Taft appears on NBC's *Meet the Press.*

DECEMBER 5

Joe Louis defends his heavyweight title by defeating Jersey Joe Walcott in a controversial split decision.

DECEMBER 6

"Near You" by Francis Craig begins the last week of its 12-week run atop *Billboard*'s "Best Sellers in Stores" chart.

DECEMBER 7

KTSP-TV begins broadcasting in St. Paul, Minnesota.

DECEMBER 8

Prince Edward, Duke of Windsor, appears on the cover of *Life* magazine.

A member of Operation Windmill poses inside a building in Antarctica. Operation Windmill is an expedition established by the Chief of Naval Operations to train personnel, test equipment, and reaffirm American interests in Antarctica.

DECEMBER 9

Dutch troops slaughter 430 boys and young men struggling for independence in Rawagede, Indonesia.

DECEMBER 10

Nine members of the "Hollywood Ten" charged with contempt of Congress surrender to a U.S. marshal.

DECEMBER 11

Radio station WLYN in Lynn, Massachusetts, begins broadcasting at 1360 AM.

DECEMBER 12

The National Security Council adopts measures that authorizes the director of the CIA to "conduct all organized Federal espionage and counterespionage operations."

DECEMBER 13

"Ballerina" by Vaughan Monroe spends the first of three weeks atop *Billboard*'s "Best Sellers in Stores" chart.

DECEMBER 14

Bill France Sr. opens discussions with professional drivers, mechanics, and car owners in Daytona Beach, Florida, to create a formal organization for stock car racing. Two months later, NASCAR is formed.

DECEMBER 15

Nelson Eddy and Jeanette MacDonald perform a version of their 1938 movie *Sweethearts* on the *Screen Guild Theater* radio program.

DECEMBER 16

William Shockley, John Bardeen, and Walter Brattain build the world's first transistor at Bell Labs in Murray Hill, New Jersey.

DECEMBER 17

WEWS, the first licensed television station in Ohio, begins broadcasting in Cleveland.

DECEMBER 18

Eddie Antar, controversial founder of the Crazy Eddie electronics chain, is born in Brooklyn, New York.

DECEMBER 19

The 1948 NFL draft is held at the Fort Pitt Hotel in Pittsburgh. Future Hall of Fame quarterbacks Bobby Layne and Y.A. Tittle are selected in the first round.

DECEMBER 20

Ralph Edwards devotes a portion of the *Truth or Consequences* radio quiz show to a visit with disabled World War II veteran Hubert C. Smith.

DECEMBER 21

The Philadelphia Eagles defeat the Pittsburgh Steelers, 21–0, in a one-game playoff to determine who wins the NFL's Eastern Division.

DECEMBER 22

Joseph Farrington, delegate to Congress for the territory of Hawaii, appears on the cover of *Time* magazine.

DECEMBER 23

Shockley, Bardeen, and Brattain demonstrate their transistor to officials at Bell Labs.

DECEMBER 24

President Truman delivers a Christmas address to
the nation at the lighting of the White House tree.

DECEMBER 25

The Road to Rio, the fourth in the "Road" series starring Bob Hope,
Bing Crosby, and Dorothy Lamour, opens in theaters nationwide.

A brochure promoting the handsome 1947 Hudson automobile.

HUDSON
FOR 1947

DECEMBER 26

One of the worst snowstorms in New York City history begins, dropping 26.4 inches of snow in Central Park over two days.

DECEMBER 27

Fittingly for the Christmas season, Norman Rockwell's *Tired Salesgirl* is featured on the cover of the *Saturday Evening Post*.

DECEMBER 28

The Chicago Cardinals win the National Football League championship, defeating the Philadelphia Eagles 28–21.

DECEMBER 29

New Yorkers continue to dig out of the snow following the blizzard.

DECEMBER 30

King Michael I of Romania abdicates his throne, placing the country under Soviet rule.

DECEMBER 31

The United Service Organizations (USO), which provided
morale and recreation services to American troops, is disbanded.
It would be revived in 1950 during the Korean War.

A warmly dressed audience awaits the lighting of the White House Christmas tree on
December 24.

Songstress Billie Holiday and companion pose for a photo in *Down Beat* magazine.

Pop Culture in 1947

The year 1947 was a monumental year in popular culture. It was when television began to make inroads in American life. At the beginning of the year, there were six commercial TV stations in the country, and none further west than Chicago. By December, there were almost 60 across America. The World Series was televised for the first time, and one show that debuted late in 1947, *Meet the Press*, remains on the air.

Movies were a major form of popular entertainment in 1947, with lighthearted fare such as *Life With Father*, *The Egg and I*, and *The Bachelor and the Bobby-Soxer* among the year's most popular films. Two films that have become beloved holiday classics, *Miracle on 34th Street* and *The Bishop's Wife*, were released in 1947. However, the end of the year saw congressional hearings into suspected Communist infiltration in Hollywood, which led to ten screenwriters and directors being blacklisted for refusing to testify, with more to follow in the next three years.

In sports, the New York Yankees won their 11th World Series title behind American League Most Valuable Player Joe DiMaggio. Boxing remained very popular, with matches from Madison Square Garden shown on TV every Friday night. Joe Louis was in the 11th year of his record-setting 13-year reign as heavyweight champion, and the lower weight classes had champions who would be household names for generations: Rocky Graziano, Sugar Ray Robinson, and Willie Pep.

A giant smiling peanut, located on the southern side of Highway 49 near Plains, Georgia. Built in 1947, it is associated with Plains native Jimmy Carter.

Top five male baby names:
1. James
2. Robert
3. John
4. William
5. Richard

Top five female baby names:
1. Linda
2. Mary
3. Patricia
4. Barbara
5. Sandra

Five radio shows that began in 1947:
The Abbott and Costello Children's Show, ABC
Family Theater, Mutual Broadcasting System
My Friend Irma, CBS
Strike It Rich, CBS
You Bet Your Life, ABC

Five radio shows that ended in 1947:
Buck Rogers in the 25th Century
Judy and Jane
Lights Out
The New Adventures of Sherlock Holmes
The Rudy Vallee Show

Popular books published:
The Pearl by John Steinbeck
Goodnight Moon by Margaret Wise Brown
Tales of the South Pacific by James Michener
All My Sons by Arthur Miller
I, the Jury by Mickey Spillane

Top five highest-grossing movies:
1. *Unconquered* ($6,100,000)
2. *The Bachelor and the Bobby-Soxer* ($5,500,000)
3. *The Egg and I* ($5,500,000)
4. *Mother Wore Tights* ($5,250,000)
5. *Life With Father* ($5,057,000)

Tommy Dorsey (left) interviews Beryl Davis for his first disc-jockey stint. Georgie Auld, Ray McKinley, Mary Lou Williams, Josh White, and others are visible in the background.

Five popular television shows:
>*Kraft Television Theatre*
>*Boxing From Madison Square Garden*
>*Kukla, Fran and Ollie*
>*Howdy Doody*
>*Meet the Press*

Five Broadway shows that opened in 1947:
>*A Streetcar Named Desire*
>*All My Sons*
>*Brigadoon*
>*Finian's Rainbow*
>*Street Scene*

Top five songs:
>1. Francis Craig, "Near You"
>2. The Harmonicats, "Peg o' My Heart"
>3. Ted Weems, "Heartaches"
>4. Ray Noble and Buddy Clark, "Linda"
>5. Tex Williams, "Smoke! Smoke! Smoke! (That Cigarette)"

Sports champions:
>Major League Baseball: New York Yankees
>National Football League: Chicago Cardinals
>All-America Football Conference: Cleveland Browns
>Basketball Association of America: Washington Capitols
>National Hockey League: Toronto Maple Leafs

Horse racing champions:
>Kentucky Derby: Jet Pilot
>Preakness Stakes: Faultless
>Belmont Stakes: Phalanx

Golf champions:
>Masters: Jimmy Demaret
>U.S. Open: Lew Worsham
>British Open: Fred Daly
>PGA Championship: Jim Ferrier

New inventions and products:
>Microwave oven
>Transistor
>Instant camera
>Acrylic paint
>Mobile phone

In April 1947 Jackie Robinson broke the baseball color line when he debuted with the Brooklyn Dodgers. Three years later he would play himself in *The Jackie Robinson Story*.

Nobel Prizes:

Physics: Sir Edward Appleton

Chemistry: Sir Robert Robinson

Physiology or Medicine: Carl Ferdinand Cori and Gerty Theresa Cori;
Bernardo Alberto Houssay (tie)

Literature: André Paul Guillaume Gide

Peace: Friends Service Council (The Quakers) and American Friends
Service Committee (The Quakers)

Pulitzer Prizes:

Public Service: The *Baltimore Sun*

Reporting: Frederick Woltman of the *New York World-Telegram*

Correspondence: Brooks Atkinson of the *New York Times*

Telegraphic Reporting (National): Edward T. Folliard of the *Washington Post*

Telegraphic Reporting (International): Eddy Gilmore of Associated Press

Editorial Writing: William H. Grimes of the *Wall Street Journal*

Novel: *All the King's Men* by Robert Penn Warren

History: *Scientists Against Time* by James Phinney Baxter III

Biography or Autobiography: *The Autobiography of William Allen White* by
William Allen White

Poetry: *Lord Weary's Castle* by Robert Lowell

Music: Symphony No. 3 by Charles Ives

Special Citations: Columbia University and the Graduate School of
Journalism

Academy Awards:

Best Picture: *The Best Years of Our Lives*

Best Director: William Wyler, *The Best Years of Our Lives*

Best Actor: Fredric March, *The Best Years of Our Lives*

Best Actress: Olivia de Havilland, *To Each His Own*

Best Supporting Actor: Harold Russell, *The Best Years of Our Lives*

Best Supporting Actress: Anne Baxter, *The Razor's Edge*

Best Original Screenplay: *The Seventh Veil,* Muriel Box and Sydney Box

Best Adapted Screenplay: *The Best Years of Our Lives,* Robert E. Sherwood

Best Original Song: "On the Atchison, Topeka and the Santa Fe" from *The
Harvey Girls* (music by Harry Warren, lyric by Johnny Mercer)

Honorary Academy Awards: Laurence Olivier, Harold Russell, Ernst
Lubitsch

Irving G. Thalberg Memorial Award: Samuel Goldwyn

Credits and Acknowledgments

David Lifton wrote text and selected images. Individual image credits are as follows.

Chapter 1. Jack Hanna—Erin Whittaker, National Park Service. Nolan Ryan—Chuck Andersen. Glenn Close—Fortune Live Media. Arnold Schwarzenegger—Bob Doran.

Chapter 2. Kaiser and Frazer ad—Graham-Paige Motors Corporation. Postal carrier—National Postal Museum. Telephone ad—Western Electric.

Chapter 3. Kitty Kallen and Doris Day—William P. Gottlieb. President Harry Truman—Library of Congress. Ernest Tubb album—unknown. Al Capone—U.S. Department of Justice. First day cover—Steve Bowbrick. Chesterfield Supper Club promo—unknown. Triple Nickel Parachute Infantry Battalion—National Archives. Army Day Parade—National Archives. Model T—marada. George Marshall—U.S. Signal Corps. *Diary of a Young Girl*—Rodrigo Galendez. Aircraft at Tempelhof airport—U.S. Air Force. Dietetic interns—National Institutes of Health. UFO Museum—AllenS. Bus station—National Archives. New Orleans postcard—unknown. Company store—Russell Lee. Fireworks at Lackland AFB—U.S. Air Force Photo / Lance Cheung. Albert Einstein—Oren Jack Turner. Liberty Tunnel—John L. Alexandrowicz, Environmental Protection Agency. Chuck Yeager—U.S. Air Force. Women at desks—Centers for Disease Control National Institute for Occupational Safety and Health. Operation Windmill—Smithsonian Archives. Hudson brochure—Hudson Motor Car Company. Tree-lighting ceremony—Abbie Rowe.

Chapter 4. Billie Holiday—William P. Gottlieb. Giant peanut—Donna Sullivan Thomson. Tommy Dorsey and Beryl Davis—William P. Gottlieb. Theater card—Jewel Pictures.